fourteen poems

Issue 7

First published in 2022 by Fourteen Publishing.
fourteenpoems.com

Edited by Ben Townley-Canning.

Design and typeset by Stromberg Design.
strombergdesign.co.uk

Proofreading and copy editing by Lara Kavanagh.
lk-copy.com

Printed by Print2Demand Ltd, Westoning, Bedfordshire, UK.

This book is sold subject to the conditions that it shall not be lent, resold, hired out or otherwise circulated without the publisher's prior consent. Copyright of the poems is owned by the individual poets named. Any republishing of the individual works must be agreed directly with the poets.

ISBN: 978-1-8383943-3-2

Hello and welcome to Issue 7 of *fourteen poems*!

As always, we've scoured the planet for the most exciting queer poems and chosen 14 of the best for you! As always, I'm so excited for you to read these poems and get to know our new batch of poets.

As always, we've tried to represent a wide array of writers, from established, award-winning poets to brand new, never-before-published ones. We also chat to most of our featured poets live on Instagram. Come join us and hear them read and chat about their work. All the details are on our Instagram page.

Your support for our little books has been mind blowing! Since our launch last year, we've published 84 queer poets, many finding a home for their poems for the first time. We're now stocked in 10 countries too and I can't wait to see us (hopefully) grow further. Together, we'll see queer poetry take over the world!

And to that end, this year will see us launching pamphlets for the first time. Keep an eye on our social channels and website for more information, but expect to see more books from us in 2022.

Thanks again for all your support! Please do share your favourite poems with us, whether on Instagram or Twitter, or by dropping me an email. I always love to hear from you all.

Enjoy the poems.

Ben Townley-Canning
Editor

Instagram: @14poems
Twitter: @fourteenpoems

contents:

- Andrew McMillan 8
- lisa luxx/Ollie O'Neill 10
- kevanté ac cash 12
- Helen Bowell 14
- Joshua Garcia 16
- Theophina Gabriel 18
- Keith Jarrett 22
- Brian Sonia-Wallace 24
- Kat Dixon 26
- Day Mattar 28
- Jim Whiteside 30
- Caleb Nichols 32
- Steven Sanchez 36
- Kelly Weber 40

Andrew McMillan is based in Manchester, UK. His debut collection *physical* (Jonathan Cape, 2015) was the first ever poetry collection to win the Guardian First Book Award. The collection also won the Fenton Aldeburgh First Collection Prize, a Somerset Maugham Award (2016), an Eric Gregory Award (2016), and a Northern Writers' Award (2014). It was shortlisted for the Dylan Thomas Prize, the Costa Poetry Award, the Sunday Times Young Writer of the Year 2016, the Forward Prize for Best First Collection, the Roehampton Poetry Prize, and the Polari First Book Prize. In 2019 it was voted as one of the top 25 poetry books of the past 25 years by the Bookseller's Association. His second collection, *playtime* (Jonathan Cape, 2018), was a Poetry Book Society Recommendation for autumn 2018, a Poetry Book of the Month in both the *Observer* and the *Telegraph*, a Poetry Book of the Year in the *Sunday Times*, and won the inaugural Polari Prize. His third collection, *pandemonium* (Jonathan Cape), was released in 2021. Andrew is a senior lecturer at the Manchester Writing School at Manchester Metropolitan University.

Instagram: @andrewpoetry
Twitter: @AMcMillanPoet

lengths

he is measuring it against the span
of his empty palm   studying the distance
between his outstretched thumb and middle finger

he is measuring it against a coke can
the SKY remote   a medium banana
its elegant curving towards the tip

he is measuring it against a microphone
testing testing   against a protein shaker
against the cracked screen of an ipad

he is measuring it against his car exhaust
the gear stick   he is measuring it against
a lamppost   this economy   his dad

he is measuring it against his own reflection
angled contrapposto   camera held just so
the self against the self   coming up short

Andrew McMillan

lisa luxx is an activist and poet of British and Syrian heritage. Her poems have been published in the *Telegraph*, the *London Magazine* and by publishers including Hachette and Saqi Books. Her work has been broadcast on Channel 4, BBC Radio 4, and TEDx. In 2021 she toured UK theatres with the show for her 60-minute poem *Eating the Copper Apple*, produced by a team of Arab women artists. Her debut collection *Fetch Your Mother's Heart* (Out-Spoken Press, 2021) is available now. Her short stories have been developed and published by Comma Press.

Instagram: @luxxy_luxx
Twitter: @lisaluxx_

Ollie O'Neill is a poet, writer, and feminist from London. She is the former UK National Youth Slam Champion, a Barbican Young Poet alumna, and has read at the Institute of Contemporary Arts, Soho Theatre, the Royal Festival Hall, Cheltenham Literature Festival, and many more. In 2019, her debut pamphlet *Ways of Coping* was published by Out-Spoken Press. In 2020, her debut full-length collection *What We Are Given* was published by Write Bloody UK. Her work explores psychiatry, misogyny, and horizontal inheritance, among other themes.

Instagram: @ollieoneill
Twitter: @olliecmoneill

little animals

i want to fuck you but the world is on fire

        & my heart, my heart, my heart.
i want. that's all there is to it, wanting, & wanting is a hard ask
when our hands are already so full of opera.
what's a body but a half-formed plea? even yours. even mine.
all of our lovers little ghosts inside of us but the world is on fire,

so how can i ask *what haunts you* and expect anything but vague gesture,
hold my hand out to the small boy of you and ask him where it hurts?
        Ollie, as the summer ends

if i were taller i'd pour out all my milk & follow
whichever path is made by its spilling

                until i outrun it

each Queer body a site of extravagance & decay
the skull of a boar on my head
as a well-meaning lady asks my pronouns again

when we make love, my hands behind my neck & shoulders birthing boyhood
this barn abandoned by stallions

                is quiet enough
                for you to hear me asking:

        luxx, as the winter begins

kevanté ac cash is a Bahamian literary artist who sometimes experiments with film. Their practice explores emotional landscapes living with mental illness, the 'triviality' of nostalgia, and the burden of bearing a queer Afro-Caribbean identity. They hold a BA in Media Journalism, an MA in Creative Writing, and have been published across the Caribbean, US and UK.

Instagram: @alexia_chatelle
Twitter: @creative_kacc

dysphoria

    break free my roots
               i am a stem of green
                            swaying

      withering

          rotted brown

    i have dreamt of being
                colors in the rainbow
    but never   of being
                myself

    i am only as free
             as freedom lends its wings
      to fly as high
               as it would let me

        break free my roots
    i am man
             woman
                    neither
      and in between

        i have dreamt of a
              boat
                    swaying the sea
          pushing to
    an answer

    i am only as free
as i am admit
    i am not

kevanté ac cash

Helen Bowell is a bisexual poet based in London, UK. Her debut pamphlet *The Barman* was published by Bad Betty Press in January 2022. Helen is a Ledbury Poetry Critic and an alumna of The Writing Squad, Roundhouse Poetry Collective, and the London Library Emerging Writers programme.

Instagram: @helen.bowell
Twitter: @helen_bowell

Object

The game is this. I smell your perfume and do not look. Nice day out. The sound of garden gnomes and Birkenstocks, other people's wind chimes. Elton John leaking out of a window. Don't let the sun go down on me. Like Sunday radio, like coffee and toast. No. I planted some rhubarb. I planted some pumpkins. Look. The sofa in a new place, a good Jenga of books. I've brought out the silk cushions we never used. Stop. The doors slam, both at once, like answers. Stop! Now I feel your crocheted blanket unravelling into spaghetti. I should have loved you and I didn't. But look at these beautiful, beautiful trousers. Pink as a little finger, promising. How you'd have hated them, how you'd have never let it go.

Helen Bowell

Joshua Garcia's poetry has appeared or is forthcoming in *Arts & Letters*, *The Georgia Review*, *Ninth Letter*, *Shenandoah*, and elsewhere. He holds an MFA from the College of Charleston and is a 2021–22 Stadler Fellow at Bucknell University.

Instagram/Twitter: @garciajoshxa

Upon Seeing a Pack of Shirtless Men Run Past Me at Golden Hour

I think, yes, of you, how I yearned for,
prayed for, believed in—I think of how belief is
its own kind of longing, & how, if broken,
so too is desire. *You came,* he said, pressing my face
in his hands, *You came, I made you come,* repeating it
as if miracle, repeating it as if saying so would make it true
again & again. To even speak the word *beauty*
sounds like a betrayal. Even as he galloped on top of me,
I thought, yes, of you, surprised to hear myself say it
—*Please*—as if prayers were ever heard from far away,
or the men in little black shorts & their measured steps
pounding the sidewalk littered with yellow leaves.

Joshua Garcia

Theophina Gabriel is an award-winning poet from Slough, UK. She is dedicated to capturing the imagination and experiences of Black LGBTQ+ women and also archiving the ways Black communities have built and continue to build powerful structures for liberation and communal care.

Instagram/Twitter: @lilaphina

Bowl

              un ti l i was
soft

un ti l i   was
s t i l l, she held me

  as i withered,

ref used to t h row   me
ou t

m ercy i cried
soft for brown earth
i was

s t i l l, she held me

i won't let you down-like here
i remember you came too, gently
& hanging ripe-like, this time
lifting all of your bruises

   itried to push past/her
wi th my skin
             but it slid,

and i screamed
and i screamed   fo r brown earth
and i screamed

and the earth came
my mother covered me
carried me out
rotten,
i could notspeak
my mother buried me

and i gave up
to the ground-like sleep

my fruiting dreams,
my aching peel,
my shivering seed
my Black.

Theophina Gabriel

Keith Jarrett is a writer, performer, and educator based in London. *Selah,* his debut poetry collection, was published in 2017 and his play, *Safest Spot in Town,* was performed at the Old Vic and aired on BBC Four.

Twitter: @keithjlondon

Bended[1]

bent back Bogle fingers: we grew from this british inversion
bent back two-by-twos, but in reverse, spiriting from the ground

sounds blend when you squint, briefly become one and then part
bend back the spine of history books and watch the black ink blur

queer (the wrong kind, a slur), or a man made of backhanders/bribes
bent, back when we were ungrown possessed only these definitions

of all bucolic english traditions seldom told in verse, I proffer just this:
the bent back bough where men queued to be caned under night sky

and so Braithwaite cry: *limbo stick is the silence in front of me*
bent back, I ache to arc towards the floor in holy quickening

come, woodsman, fling down your body's offerings!
bent back in the downpour, a lost and trembling leaf.

Keith Jarrett

---

[1] According to one theory, British dancers tend to Bogle in reverse, thrusting fingers and bodies away from their ancestral grounding, while their North American counterparts maintain a forward, downward hand motion, in keeping with other dances of the Black Atlantic.

Brian Sonia-Wallace is the West Hollywood City Poet Laureate and a national 2021 Laureate Fellow for the Academy of American Poets. He has been published in *Poets.org, Rattle, Rolling Stone, LitHub,* and the *Guardian*. Brian has spent the last decade writing poems for over 10,000 strangers based on their stories in a string of unlikely residencies, ranging from Amtrak to the Mall of America. These adventures and poems appear in Brian's memoir, *The Poetry of Strangers* (Harper Collins, 2020), which the *New York Times* called "full of optimism and wide-eyed wonder...he charms us." Brian's custom poetry business, RENT Poet, was featured on NPR's *How I Built This*. Its motto is, "everyone needs a poem".

Instagram/Twitter: @rentpoet

Cremation

When half your family dies & the other half
goes insane, you thread green lights
on summer nights toward hoodie weather,
replay future Thanksgivings at strange tables,

stuffing not your culture, you bread people
with simple butter, you dead people
ash-scattered with no funeral marker,
you run-away homecoming king

still chasing virgin dreams across continents
stale with Waffle House, Times Square
backdrop for make-up orgies, detention
in a lover's arms, *boy, sit up straight,*

wipe that grin, inherit this wreckage
we call history, we call, again & again,
nothing to say just breathing into the phone
like, *fucker I still can fog a windshield.*

I never know where I'm going.
It's out of fashion to write about loneliness,
but there, I said it, I'm lonely.
Parked in a dead man's car carrying a dead man's name,

back to an empty house with cum in my ass.
Who will re-attach my body to its language?
Who will fuck me when I live and, when I die,
tell them my choice was to be burned?

Brian Sonia-Wallace

Kat Dixon writes about relationships, race, societal norms, and queer identity. You can find her poetry in *The Rialto, Perverse, Butcher's Dog, Queerlings, Mslexia,* and forthcoming in *Re-Creation Anthology*. She recently completed an MA in Writing Poetry with Newcastle University and The Poetry School. She works with mixed media, including monochrome photographs of flesh and satirical hand sanitiser labels.

Instagram: @dixon_kat
Twitter: @katdixon2012

drips in a bucket

we're in a beer garden on Blackhorse Road / with these massive glasses / gin glasses / and you're talking about gay icons and Jacqueline Wilson and how Ellie from those Girls in Love books was definitely gay / and I say / what / how was she / and you point out the bit when she sleeps next to her best friend / smells her hair / talking about the curve of her best friend's spine / and I'm a bit drunk / squiffy my Mum would call it / and I say / yeah / but I felt that way / about some of my friends / thinking about Celeste / her strawberry blonde hair / down her back / soft skin / round the base of her breasts / when we got changed for P.E. / her white legs / when we got changed to go out / playing rounds of pool in the cine-complex / chasing boys / we kissed once / scent of damp grass and wet trainers / in a tent on a school trip / boys watching / all eyes on us / heat of fascination / and I didn't want the kiss to stop / the ice in your gin glass is melting / you've taken your sunglasses off / you're watching me / sucking on your lime / the traffic nearby feels suddenly close and far away / and I say / I can't believe Ellie was gay / poor Ellie / not knowing all this time

Kat Dixon

Day Mattar is a queer poet and performer from Liverpool, UK and the co-founder of the Queer Bodies poetry collective: 12-week writing programs for North West UK-based, queer-identifying writers. Day's pamphlet, *Springing from the Pews*, was published in May 2021 by Broken Sleep Books, where they also work part time as marketing assistant.

Instagram: @daymattarpoetry
Twitter: @daymattar

fissure

I find a star of blood after shitting
inky red streak on white tissue   from the place
designed to elasticate   snapped
from strain of *no*   taken for *harder*   *no*
called deep into anonymous face   nine flowers
splash their bright red notes against my white wall
you could say this is a jab   or an omen
but it's a geranium   cared for by me
string looped to support its slender stems
sustaining the weight of nine flared trumpets   mouths
open in song   at the window   gargling sun
which when poured down into the well of this poem
chimes back   *baby*   *darling*

                                           yes

Day Mattar

Jim Whiteside is the author of the chapbook, *Writing Your Name on the Glass* (Bull City Press, 2019), an exploration of queer love and loss in the American South. A former Wallace Stegner Fellow in Poetry at Stanford University, his recent poems have appeared in the *New York Times, Poetry Magazine, Ploughshares, the Southern Review, Best New Poets 2020,* and *Boston Review.* Originally from Cookeville, Tennessee, he holds an MFA from the University of North Carolina at Greensboro and lives in Brooklyn, New York.

Instagram: @jim_whiteside
Twitter: @whiteside_jim

Argelès-sur-Mer

Tourist town, all families and umbrellas, sunscreen
and cheap motels. The code sent to my phone, releasing

the hotel key from a machine on the wall, no front desk.
Our friend's mother, raised in Lyon, came here as a child,

recommended the stop. Early July heat. The Mediterranean's
humidity like trips to the Gulf when I was young. In the market

we eat sticky crêpes, take pictures of stacked fruit and hand-knotted
rugs. Love, will we always be childless? Sitting on the porch

of our rented room, drinking champagne from plastic cups that came
wrapped in plastic, I think, *I couldn't add anything to this.*

You go for a swim, and I watch you wading through the waves
while I sit on the beach with our things—your glasses,

the book I brought but never started. My heels make little craters.
A boy packs a bucket full of sand, turns it over to make a house.

Jim Whiteside

Caleb Nichols is a writer and musician from California, USA. His poetry has been featured in *Queerlings, Impossible Archetype*, and the *Lickety Split* among other publications, and his chapbook *Teems///\\\Recedes*, which the US-based poet Chen Chen called "a gorgeous abundance", is available now from Kelp Books. Caleb's debut solo album Ramon, a queer rock opera based on the Beatles song "Mean Mr. Mustard", is forthcoming on the label Kill Rock Stars, and he is a PhD candidate in Creative Writing at Bangor University in Wales. Caleb also owns and operates the SLO Book Bike, a queer-owned, bike-powered, pop-up bookshop in San Luis Obispo.

Instagram/Twitter: @seanickels

Bloom

Not so much a thaw
as dawn
frost
on crabgrass
giving way
to a warmth
which gently
gradually
heats
by degrees
the temperature
between us
rising
pressure
ridging
into something
like a shape
so that when
I've finally taken
measure
it just confirms
what's become
a sort
of certitude

desire

not burning
so much
as embering
not singeing
so much
as coaxing

as sunlight
pulling
open
buds

Caleb Nichols

Steven Sanchez is Queer, Latino, and currently lives in Fresno, California. His debut book, *Phantom Tongue* (Sundress Publications, 2018), was selected by Mark Doty for the Rochelle Ratner Memorial Award. His poems have appeared in *American Poetry Review, Agni, Poet Lore*, and elsewhere.

Instagram: @icarus__flies
Twitter: @steven_sanchez

Elegy for Your Southern Twang
for Clinton

Sometimes,
    like an abandoned dog,
        it slinks

back to the stoop
    of your tongue
  and waits
    for the door
        to open. For years,

you trained it
  to heel—
    you've heard
what gets said

    when whiteness
      is the only
          witness.

I know what people assumed about my accent.

Every time you return,
      you worry
      it will find you.

I know what it's like
    to fear
      your own voice,

        to hear

  a whimper
    instead of a growl,

for a kid to toss *faggot*
           like a meatball
                      minced
    with glass,
        to smile
instead of snarl
        after he spits on you
and says
        I hope you get AIDS.

Sometimes,
    we quiet ourselves

like our Shepherd
    who won't bark
        but raises
            his hackles

at the touch
        of his hind legs—
his body recoils,
    recalls
                the man who slammed him
            against a wall.

Once, we saw a stray huddled in the rain.

He ran before we reached him.

We tell ourselves he's   resilient.

He doesn't need to be rescued.

Steven Sanchez

Kelly Weber is the author of the debut poetry collection *We Are Changed to Deer at the Broken Place* (Tupelo Press, 2022) and the chapbook *The Dodo Heart Museum* (dancing girl press, 2021). Their work has appeared or is forthcoming in *Hayden's Ferry Review, Southeast Review, The Missouri Review*, and elsewhere. She holds an MFA from Colorado State University and has been a finalist for the Omnidawn Open, as well as a Pushcart nominee.

Instagram/Twitter: @kellyweberpoet

Ode to the Drift Glass Necklace My Friend Gave Me

she said it's good / when you can finally find the words for your queerness isn't it / and it was like finding finchsong braided in my marrow / for the very first time / everyone needs someone / to do that for them / give them permission for a more honest language / to live / like every blue and green bottle sawing the lake shore / of my family's blood / of every daughter who drank rat poison or liquor / could be softened to wrists / accreting sun blades into mercy / every secret we sank in the water / like forcing shut the teeth of a trap / -ped animal / for years I have tried to fit / all the pieces of my gender / inside me / almost all female / but still there has been / something else / speaking out of me when I'm anemic / rusting into rumor of moon / fable cored girl who hated being called sir / then offered an apology wrapped in a stare at my breasts / and a Jesus bookmark / hated being called ma'am by strangers / avoided mirrors while naked / dressing as a skeleton or gender ambiguous for Halloween / cutting my hair shorter and shorter / gender as girl with snake in her mouth / one breast cut off to let gush from it / a fork tongued doe / a language made out of everything that doesn't fit / because I want to be as beautiful / as my friends think I am / when I can't get my hair cut for a long time / I hate the woman who stares out of me / like a long denied heir / of marrow and glass / but I can make it through waiting / one more day / because my friends say / my whole queer self is beautiful / because my best friend / makes me feel soft enough / to live inside these long lacy sleeves / draw my knees up to my chest / tender skin and black tights stretched taut / like I could finally let someone / like her sleep against my side / like this / gently breathing together / platonically / in our bodies / it has taken me this long / to let the sharptoothed animal / of whatever gender I am / live inside me like this / watching the stone on my chest / bounce in time with my pulse / like my name / means both green / and any gender / I'm born to / thigh teeming into rain / and pubic hair / ovaried meadow / the words I use for myself wide enough to hold / agave bloom and panic / grass perennial / coneflower uncorseting my pronouns / into greening tongues

Kelly Weber

Enjoyed these poems?

Scan the QR code below to check out our other issues and save 20% on a subscription by using the code **BACKPAGE** on our website.